Myrrh, Mothwing, Smoke

Tupelo Press Chapbooks

Barbara Tran, *In the Mynah Bird's Own Words*
Selected by Robert Wrigley

David Hernandez, *A House Waiting for Music*
Selected by Ray Gonzalez

Mark Yakich, *The Making of Collateral Beauty*
Selected by Mary Ruefle

Joy Katz, *The Garden Room*
Selected by Lisa Russ Spaar

Cecilia Woloch, *Narcissus*
Selected by Marie Howe

John Cross, *staring at the animal*
Selected by Gillian Conoley

Polina Barskova, *This Lamentable City*
Edited by Ilya Kaminsky, translated by the editor
    with Kathryn Farris, Rachel Galvin and Matthew Zapruder

Stacey Waite, *the lake has no saint*
Selected by Dana Levin

Brandon Som, *Babel's Moon*
Selected by Aimee Nezhukumatathil

Kathleen Jesme, *Meridian*
Selected by Patricia Fargnoli

Myrrh, Mothwing, Smoke

Erotic Poems

Edited by Marie Gauthier and Jeffrey Levine

Tupelo Press
North Adams, Massachusetts

Myrrh, Mothwing, Smoke
Collection copyright 2012 by Tupelo Press; individual poems
are copyrighted by their authors. All rights reserved.

Library of Congress Cataloging-in-Publication Data

Myrrh, mothwing, smoke : erotic poems / edited by Marie Gauthier and Jeffrey
Levine. ~ First paperback edition.
    pages cm
Includes bibliographical references.
ISBN 978-1-936797-27-1 (pbk. original : alk. paper)
1. Erotic poetry, American. I. Gauthier, Marie, 1971- editor of
compilation. II. Levine, Jeffrey, 1949- editor of compilation.
PS595.E76M97 2013
811'.60803538~dc23

2013005078

First paperback edition: December 2012.

Cover and text designed by Rose Carlson.
Cover painting: "She Arranges Her Hair," by Corinne Galla, 2009.
From the series After the Kiss. Watercolor, 4 x 6 inches.
Used by permission of the artist. (www.etsy.com/shop/CGallaFineArt)

Tupelo Press, P.O. Box 1767, North Adams, Massachusetts 01247
Telephone: (413) 664-9611 / Fax: (413) 664-9711
editor@tupelopress.org / www.tupelopress.org

Tupelo Press is an award-winning independent literary press that
publishes fine fiction, nonfiction, and poetry in books that are a joy
to hold as well as read. Tupelo Press is a registered 501(c)3 nonprofit
organization, and we rely on public support to carry out our mission
of publishing extraordinary work that may be outside the realm of the
large commercial publishers. Financial donations are welcome and
are tax deductible.

"Take this body."

– *from* Aubrey Ryan's
O Honey, Won't You Rock My World Up North

Contents

IV Editors' Selections

Editors' Note:

In 2007, the Tupelo Press Poetry Project was established to provide poets and creative writing teachers with engaging prompts and challenging provocations for writing new poems.

The Winter 2012 edition of the Poetry Project celebrated Valentine's Day with a simple challenge: write a stunningly good erotic poem. Be bad. Be good and bad. To our delight, that challenge was met and then some.

Sensual, witty, cerebral — the results are this anthology, modest in size only, which includes the winners plus our favorites of the submissions.

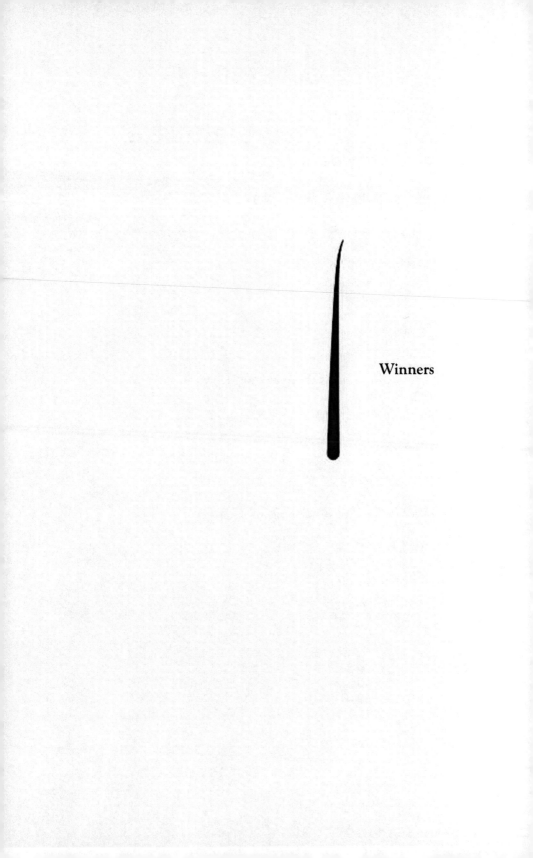

Winners

Dialogue with Gaps

These meadows themselves open, brush the horizon

and was the —
>*yes*

it were she says
>*it were what*

she says he's sorry
>*same old*

he says she's right
>*damn straight*

she says she arrives
>*and why not*

Some meadows flayed by wind, pinned by trees

she says she remembers
>*sorry*

she says she liked it
>*right*

she says what of it

Arrive then, riding between trees, legs clasped

what he says
>*don't*

the matter was her

These trees in these meadows green at the tips

>*her nipples were*
>*her eyes were*
>*her hair was*
>*her mouth formed*
>*her thighs opened*

That grass coarse against which some lay back

his hair black
his hands spread
his lips hard
his eyes closed
his mouth wide

Among trees overhead leaves curl like hair

observe she says
catch me
what he says
can't
where he is
disappeared
matter she says
and he rides on

A meadow, distant now, each line of grass arrayed against another

her green fingers reach
he rides
she reaches further
he rides

O Honey, Won't You Rock My World Up North

The snow will go for days, our road
keep trackless, and the lamplight
spill then stay. You're gold
in wool and overalls; you're a sight

to see: my man. One pear, one pound
of chestnuts in a paper bag, one kettle set
to burst. I'm smooth and round;
I'm a shallow bowl of oil: so sweet

for flame. Bring shovel, bring
salt and light a match to me — my bones
will melt. Honey, ring
me in garland: I'm a festival. Our home

is in the branches of jack pine. Our bedposts hum
like hives. Take this body. We'll make a wet thaw come.

Hypothesis, Proof

A week of nonnegotiable fantasy, days
of unmovable image — in a locked room,

against a door, in front of the window.

I, of course, am wearing a skirt, stockings
holding onto my thighs. You look

and then look down. You think

what you think. There's only this table
between us — a slight expanse

of wood and steel, file cabinets,

note-taking. You rely on me
and I you, not to. But I'm undependable

with the right kind of pressure.

I look outside at the land you love
clearing its throat, preparation

for singing. We have an understanding.

A bridge arches over the river, river
rises to meet it, pigeons fly out

from the dark underneath, and starlings

rise and fall in parabolic sweeps, glissandos
drawn from architecture and math, music

almost impossible to play.

Honorable Mentions

Kiss

Before buttons and unbuttoning,
before the lock fell to the key
or the prelude gave away parts of the opus

you had your practice, an adept,
you kept your X'd map of our coordinates

you went on setting your little traps of pillows.

I can't flatter you sufficiently:
your indecent shine (like glimpsing a zipper)
your tongue loosing words off what they cover.
In broad daylight you smack of the ample bed
over a truck hood or luncheonette table.
I'd have been so upright without you —
kinks all still in my spine —
and no touching faith in the seasonal.

Naughty: the lines you blur but won't erase.
Tan line, lip line, language of a contract.

Strewn softness swamping the tooth,
balm to the wound, and wound giver, and wound,

you won't let us pretend
wet belongs to the other element.

Frond

Legs, pressed together, keep a shadow there.
The dark between thighs,
another variation of the frond.

                *

Sometimes I push my cock
between my legs to see what difference likes.
I'll yearn for space
inside me, the strange
fullness of entry, conjunctions.

                *

The photo on my wall.
A stranger's smooth skin, four lines
converging to her sex,
beside a postcard
of the fossil palm, dark hand in stone, evidence
of ancient lushness in the present's desert,
how likeness found or crafted makes desire
no longer secret
but sanctity.

                *

Outside, above the river,
what flew then flies now:
dragonfly, kingfisher.

Water striders press down like fingers.

A wing is spread. Feathers part.

Our bodies are fans that open.

*

Force invented the frond, as the frond
begets force, and rain falls
or slickness rises to glisten surfaces in time,
and light arrives on all of it.

How I want these shapes and how
these shapes want themselves.

Lepidoptera Nocturne

We climb each other like a rock face, grab
at ears, nipples for holds. Stacked limbs

are cairn, monument. The insects
spiral round our column, the false eyes:

violet, cerulean, navy repeating.
Not the familiar Monarch flit

and go, sidewalk moment landers, little
tickle on the nose or forearm in the Butterfly

Rainforest, a children's museum.
They bump the second-story

glass until it gives, stream in the window
the night you cry in my bed, powder of the wings

mixes with brackish lines on your face. They black
out the lights, the thread-thin antennae touching

my hair, your hands in it.
Exhausted, they quiet. The largest lands

on your chest, flattens itself like a collapsed
circus tent. Stripe upon bright stripe, quilt

of jewel. Then, your hands folding mine into
letters, signing to me with my own fingers,

as if even shouted I might not hear.

Errata

This is what he fells me.
He's never been with anyone so errata,
how he bloves all the blings I do to whim.
That's the vermouth.
He says hell be there forever.
I coo the girl fling, mold on.
He rumbles.
And there he flows, out of my wife.

I still steal his touch, his misses,
want to fall him, come up with any season.
He left his thanks in the hamper,
his iplod in my fish tank.
I want to bring them clover to him.
Take me whack.
I want you lack.

This is what I drink.
I'm just a tool for love
as the song throws,
a drool, a ghoul,
a pool for blove.

Aubade for Peter Pan

He slips his shadow from the drawer, sees it fall, a rivulet of breath, to the floor. His skin leaps up, as if to claim it. He breathes the bitter tang of sweat and years, sees again where deepest wounds have stained it. Thinks for a moment of rolling it up again, closing the drawer and flying on, without the shadow or the girl, the mess of it all. But once she says, *I'll stitch it back on,* once she begins at the heel, he knows he's lost his chance to refuse the pinprick of bone-white needle held soft in her hand. He tries to hold still. The piercing of skin, the thin blade of her warmth on his as she pulls the soul-thread taut, deep like a root. The edge of lost shadow on found skin, dark as a plum. Her light and depths now woven into his. Their shadows, always telling truth but slantwise. He decides to stay here in this ever-land. It feels like home.

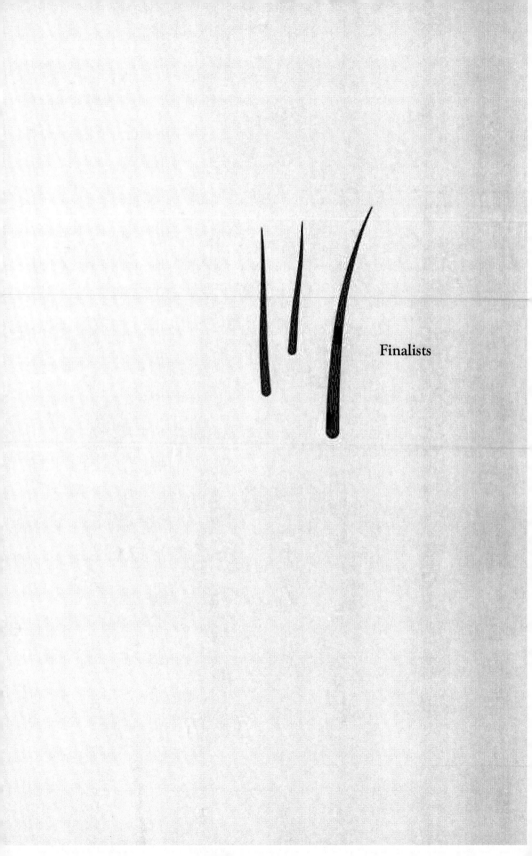

Finalists

Ether

Even as I lie here, in this cavern,
on this wide bed, half-empty now,
staring into the white
of the vaulted ceiling, in this echo
on the edge of Toledo, hollow
in this corner of Ohio,
two thousand miles from where she,
in California, in the clutter of a crowded room I cannot
imagine, a room I've never seen,
lies asleep on the featherbed I gave her, deep
in another life, another time,
in her mother's house in Altadena,
even as I lie here waiting
for my life, for ours, sometimes the myrrh
of her hair, the mothwing of her cheek,
they come to me. If I close my eyes,
the flute of her murmured I love you, the smoke
of her eyes come, her nectar sheen,
sometimes the iron tang of her
clitoris beneath my tongue, she comes
to me, two thousand miles folded
into a breath
between us, sometimes her mouth,
her tongue, her palms, sometimes
her fingers, come the heat, the slow-sweet spasm,
through the ether, the embrace,
till my eyes open once again
into this white vault.

On the Merits of Lingerie

My friend has her breasts removed:
I rediscover lace. Lady-in-waiting
bedside, I keep vigil as sutures settle,
thrust two forearms under blanketed
knees so she can scoot upright,
sip meatball soup fetched from cafeteria.
Back home, dig an ancient teddy
from the crypt of forgotten garments
and glide into pitch satin,
remembering how I'd lost my way
weaving back from the cafeteria,
self-recriminations concerning vanity,
the body's tyranny. Brand new hospital
and many rooms empty. Fresh carpet,
paint — pristine wings ignorant
of suffering to come: incessant thumbs
pressed to morphine buttons. My friend was dozing
when I found her again, a few wisps
of gray dream fallen to one side
of her smooth crown. That night
my husband brandished his flesh
and I fell on it, more in love suddenly
than I'd recalled, reaching
down for the little curtain:
I swept aside black silk and let death enter.

The Last Time

I drink alone in the bar of the Peninsula,
apple martinis,
thinking of a man I asked to bed.
What if I said I loved you?

You make me feel gentle,
he said,
as he dressed and walked away.

Liaison

The moment he took my body to his, the world was water. I heard
rain, rain on the sidewalk of Passage de Flandre, rain on the
boulevards, rain on the tin roofs, a thrumming so hard it could only
be made of softness. I saw trees slick, bare and black in the showers
sheeting the city. And one tree I saw clearly, a silhouette of elm.
One branch, one twig, I saw. How a drop of water clung and in its
orb a shine, as from a streetlamp. How a second drop fell on the
first, and together they swelled so full they quivered — it was all they
could do not to break, to hold on. And heavy, too heavy to bear
their union, they fell to the sidewalk beneath the tree, not knowing
what became of themselves —

Darla Himeles

Stopping by the Old Classroom

Empty desks smeared with pencil,
air sticky, redolent of your morning
buttered toast.

To think how I taught
while reading you in the air
between students —

your careless walk,
slight tilt of chin, quick eyes,
body long against my desk.

To think our flames seared this space —
old furniture melted
like your folds, delicate between teeth.

I Sip a Martini

You talk about notes —
A minor 7th and playing the frets.

I'm looking at your crotch;
tight denim, orange threads, steel rivets.

Something hard in my throat.
I study your knee,

swung improvisationally
over the bar stool.

I swallow,
and surface

Pianissimo!

To two olives with pimento,
side by side, Adam & Eve

on a toothpick,
floating high above the gin.

(now we're older the body worship turns)

– after Feng Menlong's "Idiot Thoughts,"
translated by Tony Barnstone

now we're older the body worship turns
now the erotic inside out in some ways better not

to consume you so hard the needle pricking the arm
for the sedative now the teaspoon of sugar thought

slowly planned in the morning for night tea this
the stage of gentle past only certain kinds of peril

yet when you are away my thoughts hurry you home
my nose fitting your neck's hollow for the garland

of leaves your self still to me as on childhood's
Block Island beach overturning the white clam shell

the surprise bolt of purple wampum what Native
Americans fashion into sacred beads now your beloved

loons are back circling the lake and the splash of white
face paint reminds me of chalk how the infinite stars

will be out soon even they dots on a board an equation
one day outdated pinpricks kisses on skin

Give and Take

In Rangiroa, on the balcony of our *fare*,
I was fading like the moon, thinning

like the call of the frigate bird
in the palms

when you took me
in, behind you, at the railing

and I gave long
and unexpectedly

because of your giving —
our mouths taking in

the molten air, our ears
taking in the wind,

the tide taking in
sand, giving back

waves, sandbars
before darkened water.

IV

Editors' Selections

MexiRican Love

for Mike

My silk turns to seda,
as is esta nena se da
por completa, and you
trill your tongue to my
pleasure. I did not teach
you to say my name
in Spanish, but somehow
your fingers learned
to trace memories
of concrete laughter
and ice cream trucks
on the balmiest of
whenevers. Mi amor,
te quiero desde no se
cuando. Orale. Wepa.

A Royal Coachman Trout Lure Sent As Courtship Gift

Miniature aggressor in tinsel, tippet, fluff,
perched so lightly on my hand
that the hook doesn't prick.
(If I blow a kiss, it flies.)
Lets my finger stroke its wings —
folded up, as if for take off —
wings snipped from mallard feather
and the coppery hairy body
wrapped in peacock herl
that vaguely makes me squirm.

I have to say "I'm touching it"
to feel a thing at all.
(In herl alone a warning:
the feather carries barbs.)
Next, floss, wound tight, like I am,
and splayed pheasant-tippet tail.
For he is so bold, this love who sent it,
that he declares his recipe for the lure.
There's something godlike, he writes,
in selling these illusions.

Attractor patterns have names like Humpy,
Stimulator, Wooly Bugger. The Royal Coachman
isn't meant to imitate a real fly
but provoke a strike
from fish not used to being pressured.

Imagine the cast! The clear water wicking
up past hook to the barely alighted body.
Then the other body, iridescent, rising.

Say It

the way a flower says
calyx, style and pistil, the petals
a bright digression, lure
to business below decks, below stairs,
beneath stars in the vaulted
apse of the flower's throat —
Gynoecium (woman's house) —
where the perennially unspent
ovary, so like the uvula
clicking imperceptibly with breath,
steadily reinvents itself, embroiders
and divides, until everything
in the poem (the flower) speaks
to everything else, spinning
and splitting until the tale comes
true enough to tell.

Eating an Orange 1348

First flies then crows then pigs
pulling apart the carcass in front of her cottage.
She can't cross without stepping over
the braids of its intestines.
Tries to remember the orange
its shallow pores and round weight
warm as a breast in her palm. He said

It won't keep.

Cut it with his knife
juice spreading on her table, a sticky stain
the white flesh of opened skin, the seeds
the smell of it, the brilliant juicy chambers
how they sprayed as he tore them apart with his fingers
the crushed pulp tart enough to tighten her cheeks.
The color. The taste again. The color and the smell.
When the flies came, he said

We can't stay.

The plague came with the flies. He got sick
then everyone else, her mother, his parents
the mercer, the potter, the abbot, the smith.
She pinches closed her nose.
Tries to remember the orange.

Boys, Friends

Body farmers,
                boyfriends,
           buff friends, the boys who
feel nothing for me, friends who are boys,
                    and it's all the same,
       boys, friends, bottom feeders,
           the best of frantic feelings,
               bordering on freezing, and
     beyond the fast lane it's all the same,
          a briar filled with foxes,
       burnt fossils under tar, boys on fire, and
           who will bring figs
                 to the broken fire inside me?

Still Life of Masturbation

She, with the poignancy of an uncovered grave,
sits — pale lipped — bathed in the window's filtered light.
She clutches the Virgin Mary to her breasts, as each
saintly wax eye melts into a misshapen pool.

Beneath the candle's staccato flicker, her shoes
gleam like tigers, threatening to stain the tiled floor.
With abeyant lust, she feels her fingers encase
her waist as it sweats petals against her palms.

She imagines a world where her hands will evoke
unforeseen notes of dignity with each curling
knuckle — & where her musical physique will fall
apart at her fingernail's own unguided graze.

Portrait Post-Orgasm

Gasoline mist wraps gauze around your lips.
You hear your throat expel notes that simmer
the way rattlesnakes whisper through the sand.
With fingertips like quivering lilacs,
pollen stains your cheeks. Jade dew accumulates
beyond your marrow as light begins to bloom.

You flicker between windows like a falling branch.
Coral static engulfs your skin, leaving only your thighs
exposed as you run your tongue across the contours
of your own enamored face.

New

Dip of your collarbone,
slant of your thigh, the dusting
of moles on your upper arm.
I chart you slow.
Expanse of your back,
stepping stones of spine,
how your edges blend
under flesh. Your wrist bones
slide under my fingers,
a different combination; your hands
in mine, a different lock.
The sheen on your skin
almost reflects me. My fingertips
graze your beard, and I try to imprint
the stubble below your lip.
Your smell is like a new mineral,
your taste bright like pink salt.
You are my just-opened trunk,
tree-top perch, high desert,
cupboard of spices, spring-planted garden.
My favored foreign land.

On Roasting

Hefting a chicken and holding a string,
your voice returns to me unbidden:
"Please," against my neck that long, slick
afternoon. I shut out your whisper and stuff
butter and garlic down the chest cavity.
Cleaned, plucked, cold weight on my fingers,
it needs salt — but, kaleidoscopic, those crystals
resolve into your face jeweled in sweat — saltier
than the fowl I grip, to forget. Unresponsive, its spine
ignores these final insults: I tie down
its small elbows, twine a slow unwinding
(your scarf curls slowly off your neck, wind-blown)
hunched over chicken, sprinkling limbs with thyme,
the oven's hot, my will — that bird — has flown.

Reflection

Your effervescent breath, your lips, still drinking
the night in, your eyes contained the restaurant
for a second, then turned back, I was thinking
this is never really the life we want:

It is not that the confetti of summer dresses
multiplied by millions of mirrors and doors
could ever let up, nor something in silver dishes,
like gold duck, nor in white, like blood: We are

what we are, not what we order; it is normal
to be thirsty, and mortal, waiting to be fed
from the deafening rhythm of the floor, it is all

what we make of it, the miracle-making bed
of lettuce, the wine and flesh, the chef's surprise,
the check, the coffee color of your eyes.

Love Poem for Christer

You can hammer crooked nails,
Catch the grandfather bass,
You can make me laugh.

You could persuade a moose
To tickle you in the morning.

When you are wrong,
I am nervous.
Clouds drown.

I'd rather have the earth wrinkle.

You can make up a song
And sing it so I'm lazy.

Your calloused hands feel good.
When your face gets red you taste good.

You could make a pine tree sorry
It littered needles.

It seems safe to go to sleep when you are there.

When you are gone,
The moon is sharp edged
And the wind chokes.

You could finesse the bones
Out of the pickerel.

You can make me glad,
when I think we will die,
You can make me glad,
Like the loon
With the bass
In her belly.

adrenaline

then remembering, then guessing, then cautioned, then
nothing given up would close. i had washed two years
from my hands, relinquished your coming to requiem.
there was no such reason to try to pretend where i was.
windowless and without filler interference, the hallway
tightened in the entirety of SORTIE emergency lights.
as orange as Israel, they all were sinless contradiction:
warning and wanting, as you alone were a second exit.
no bunked beds, no broken hinge, no television encores.
no mixed messages, no pretext, no doubt and no sleep.
the garden of ceremony, trips and prayers which led us
here, led no more, finished nothing. you and i had not
yet stumbled into the truth, when we laid on the world
an altar of things hidden within the vertical, exposed
in the horizontal. your body became the environment:
the radiator, the foreign escape routes, the fire alarm —
an offering of emergency, of now or never. reading the
scriptures of threads from your clavicle to your thighs,
i delayed letting go. my leaving undone, as the exit in
you was endless. still remembering, still guessing, still
cautioned, still nothing given up will close. a naked eve
of wide open space, wide open space, wide open space.

In

in and in in
distant person in ignition
cringe blink motion skin
agony beckon binge brink
window alignment acquaintance win
sin lesson rinse rinse innocent

inner inch inch innocent
wince winter becoming in
stand-in wrinkle potions win
heavens ink igni- igni- ignition
swing peeking and brink
inevitable hinge inevitable skin

insouciant second skin skin
spring prince innocent
pin pin vermillion brink
something tingle bring ring in
Berlin Boston since ignition
Belgian mandolins cinch win

open dinner instant win
injections spring rejection skin
genuine moccasin gin ignition
instinct fingers pinch innocent
hint squint sink skin in
peppermint footprint brink brink

inquiry absinthe inspection brink
finials crinolines spin win win
mannequins begin begging in
Linzer insy Lindy skin
masculine feminine innocent
harlequin jessamine ignition

Lincoln ermine kin ignition
larynx adrenalin into brink
island innocent innocent
spin and flinch wind win
instill inspire flint skin
succinct succinct succinct in

innocent sing sing win
ignition cushion piston skin
indigo brink and in in and in.

The Two-Girl Tether

I sleep in your old socks and want
        our two old rooms. I want

your thrift-store slips and black mascara
        ground into my sheets. Far north,

I miss my skin. I wear it like a guard-rail
        clanging through the wreck; I wear it

like it's scales, but every night I'm sticky
        as a cherry drop and deep, deep

red between my layers. You'd blush
        to see. I'm sure you're nearer

than I think. I think your hips still follow me
        down hallways, and your belly is a kite

tied to my wrist. Come here. I'll wear you out
        against the last gray stretch of March.

The Body Donation

About to leave the lab, and eager
(Dear) to hear your latest serenade.
An undertaker rings. Offers me
a body (not yours)—Miss Gracie Hart

from Darlington. I ask you: How much
more like Love can Death address herself?
(The gamma distribution counts the
waiting till it dies). What shall I name

this game of joy anticipated,
grief delivered? "Dadaist?" Surreal?
You know as well as I. We all die.
(Or was it Miss Darling from Hartsville?)

Can bodies freight the weight — or minds — of
love, too much like death, too much like love?

Tripped

Naked, you posed on a New Mexico bridge. Forged
into the twatterlight along the Río Grande's gorge,

your body, sacred sculpture, flawless & geason,
a prime cut of bouffage for your zaftig muskin.

I brinch you, drink to you, frike lusty half-marrow,
man of my morning, my steamy eveglom pharaoh.

I swingle in your presence: Shaboom, life's a sweven,
a ya-da-da-da-da-da California cream beach heaven

where you lay next to an elephant seal, made a wreck
of that harem master turned carked, neurotic melsh-dick.

You doused the garboil of slippery breeding attempts,
put a stop to that briny, leathery doo-wop fleshment.

And in Incan *tierra* when a June *luna* smicked the sky,
you canoed me to paradise, your fine farlies stupefied,

your amorets oozing, pouring sweet Andean pulpatoons
into me & ancient Chimborazo's swelling crater lagoons.

You rock me, sweetheart, come framble, come prangle.
O let me grubble your black, frim crisples. Let's tangle.

Law of Attraction

Under metallic winter sky
deep woods open to the lake's
thick lid of ice spread like
grey frosting. In a clearing

you are poised over stump
of pine, axe raised, plaid bulk
of coat stretched across broad
shoulders. With ears flushed

red from breath and will
you lift the blade high,
then arc it down fast to
cleanly split the yellow

heart. A crack bounces
off frozen water. You bend
down until plaid and each
layer beneath inches up

to reveal coffee skin and
womanly hips. Startling, this
desire to cleave, to be hoisted
by the heft of your steady aim.

Drought

The crows, they
circle, dragging their
wretched shadows,
and light tiptoes
gingerly
as day trips into moon
and fields sprawl
in both directions —
bleached; fallow;
studded with want.
Look here,

I am the thirst;
I am the stubble in the field.
Lull me,
I am wanting.
Sink your fingers deep
and fondle my seed.

Coax me.
Wet me.
Color me wheat.

Kim Triedman

Siren

She has a pillbox, he said,
but hair like flame
spills down her back. Otherwise
there was a hatchet in her car, and
next: that ruby patch
of poison ivy. It was

too much, he said — her hair
spills down her back,
words fall from her like bits
of burning ash. At midday just

a windless calm.
Somewhere out there
he hears the wail of a siren,
and he steps outside,
barefoot,
without thinking.

Live Bait

Crickets pull the impossible night from a corner.
The earth's ore rises to the surface,
red worms and crawlers braiding loam.
I lace my hand into bodies, smooth, moist.

Behind an old garage, a pile of mulch offered
this extravagance — steam rose from rot,
worms fingered the surface into living darkness.
I leaned against the wall, your palms a cold shock

on my hips as you pushed my shirt up my ribs.
Our lips so close breath was a strand of silver
between us. Crickets insisted — your hand
sliding the narrow between jeans and stomach,

your breasts as much moonlight as I would ever need.
How can we deny the brown bodies, leg singing against leg.
The rich earth clings to my fingers, my nostrils flare,
I think of the silky movement of our tongues.

Contributors

Cynthia Rausch Allar received her M.F.A. from (and met her wife at) Spalding University. Published recently in *Naugatuck River Review, Evening Street Review, Off the Rocks, Paper Street, Bloom,* and *Allegorica: A Journal of Medieval and Renaissance Literature,* she lives in Pasadena, California, with her wife and their cat extraordinaire, Hermione.

Li Yun Alvadaro is a Puerto Rican poet and educator. In 2009, she received an Academy of American Poetry Prize and one of her poems was selected for inclusion in *where the wind turns: The Red Moon Anthology 2009.* Li Yun is currently a doctoral candidate in Fordham University's English department, where she has helped coordinate Fordham's Poets Out Loud reading series. She lives in New York City. (www.liyunalvarado.com)

Michelle Bitting has work published or forthcoming in *The American Poetry Review, Prairie Schooner, Narrative, Linebreak,* and others. Poems have appeared on the website Poetry Daily and she has been the Weekly Featured Poet on the website Verse Daily. Thomas Lux chose her manuscript *Good Friday Kiss* as the winner of the DeNovo First Book Award (C & R Press, 2008). *Notes to the Beloved* won the 2011 Sacramento Poetry Center Award and was recently published (Sacramento Poetry Center Press, 2012). She holds an M.F.A. in Poetry from Pacific University, Oregon. (www.michellebitting.com)

Paula Brancato is a first-generation Sicilian-American poet. One of the first women executives on Wall Street, she is also a film and music producer and strategic planner for hedge funds, money managers, and the World Bank. She earned her M.B.A. at the Harvard Business School and is a graduate of Hunter College and Los Angeles Film School. She teaches screenwriting and poetry at the University of Southern California's Master of Professional Writing Program and Stony Brook Southampton College. In 2011, her third chapbook, *For My Father,* was released by Finishing Line Press.

Lisa Coffman has received fellowships for her poetry from the National Endowment for the Arts, the Pew Charitable Trusts, the Pennsylvania Council on the Arts, and Bucknell University. Her first book of poetry, *Likely,* won the Stan and Tom Wick Poetry Prize and was published by Kent State University Press.

Christopher Cokinos is the author of two books of literary nonfiction, *Hope Is the Thing with Feathers: A Personal Chronicle of Vanished Birds* and *The Fallen Sky: An Intimate History of Shooting Stars*, both from Tarcher/Penguin. His poems, essays, and reviews have appeared in such venues as *Poetry, The Volta, High Desert Journal, Shenandoah,* the *Los Angeles Times, Science,* and *High Country News.* He teaches in the M.F.A. program at the University of Arizona, where he is also an affiliated faculty member with the Institute of the Environment.

Gilliam Cummings's poems have appeared or are forthcoming in *Boulevard, The Laurel Review, Colorado Review, The Cincinnati Review, Quarterly West,* and other journals. Her chapbook *Spirits of the Humid Cloud* was published by Dancing Girl Press in 2012. She is a graduate of Sarah Lawrence College's M.F.A. program and teaches poetry workshops at a hospital.

Amy Dryansky's first book, *How I Got Lost So Close To Home,* was published by Alice James Books, and individual poems have appeared in a variety of anthologies and journals, including, *Orion, New England Review, Harvard Review,* and *make/shift.* She currently works for a regional land trust, teaches in the Writing Program at Hampshire College, and writes about what it's like to navigate the territory of mother/artist/poet at her blog, Pokey Mama (http://amydryansky. wordpress.com/). Her second book, *Grass Whistle,* is forthcoming from Salmon Poetry.

Darla Himeles, a degree candidate in the M.F.A. Program in Poetry and Poetry in Translation at Drew University, lives and works in coastal Maine. Her poems and poetry reviews have recently appeared in *5 AM, Great River Review, Spillway,* and *Pleiades.*

Anna Claire Hodge is a first year Ph.D. student in poetry at Florida State University. She received her M.F.A. from Virginia Commonwealth University in 2010. She was a finalist for the 2012 Copper Nickel Poetry Contest, and her work has appeared in *Hayden's Ferry Review, Breakwater Review, Makeout Creek,* and *Blue Earth Review.*

Joel F. Johnson is a self-employed businessman living in obscurity in Concord, Massachusetts. He is a member of the Concord Poetry Center and has attended the Colrain Manuscript Conference. His poems have been published in *Blackbird, Grey Sparrow Journal, Salamander, A River and Sound Review* and other journals.

Janet R. Kirchheimer is the author of *How to Spot One of Us* (Clal, 2007), a collection of poems about the Holocaust. Her work has appeared in *Atlanta Review, Connecticut Review, Lilith,* and *Natural Bridge,* and in the anthologies *99words* and *Villanelles.* She was awarded a Certificate of Appreciation from the 261st Signal Brigade for her work in the 2009 Multi-National Forces Days of Remembrance Holocaust Memorial Service held at Camp Victory in Baghdad, Iraq.

Conley Lowrance began writing poetry after an aborted career in punk rock. His endeavors in writing led him to the University of Virginia, where he recently received his B.A., majoring in poetry writing. His writings have appeared in publications such as *Gadfly, Counterexample Poetics, The Virginia Literary Review,* and *The Last Romantics.* Currently, Conley works for tattooed women in a local soul food restaurant and spends large portions of time grooming his four cats.

Amy MacLennan has been published in *Hayden's Ferry Review, River Styx, Cimarron Review, Painted Bride Quarterly, Folio, Rattle,* and *Linebreak.* Her chapbook *The Fragile Day* was released from Spire Press in the summer of 2011, and her chapbook, *Weathering,* was published by Uttered Chaos Press in early 2012.

Lea Marshall is an M.F.A. candidate at Virginia Commonwealth University, where she is also Interim Chair and a producer in the Department of Dance and Choreography. Her work is forthcoming in *Hayden's Ferry Review* and has been published in *Miracle Monocle, Moon Milk Review, diode,* and *Anderbo.com.* In addition, she is a freelance dance writer and critic, and she helps run Ground Zero Dance. She lives in Richmond, Virginia, with her husband and daughter.

Stephen Massimilla is a poet, critic, and painter. He has received the Stephen F. Austin State University Press Prize for *The Plague Doctor in His Hull-Shaped Hat* (2013); the Bordighera Poetry Prize for *Forty Floors from Yesterday* (2002); the Grolier Prize for *Almost a Second Thought;* a Van Rensselaer Award, selected by Kenneth Koch; an Academy of American Poets Prize; and four Pushcart Prize nominations. Massimilla holds an M.F.A. and a Ph.D. from Columbia University and teaches at Columbia University and The New School.

Mary Ann Mayer's newest work is in *Salamander* and *The Providence Journal*. She is an outreach volunteer with Ocean State Poets and a member of the Origami Poems Project. She has published one book of poems, *Telephone Man* (AuthorHouse, 2005). She is an occupational therapist living in Sharon, Massachusetts, with her husband and their dog, Ezra Hound.

Barbara Mossberg is Poet in Residence for the City of Pacific Grove, California, and founder and host of the weekly radio program Poetry Slow Down on KRXA 540 AM (podcast at BarbaraMossberg.com). She is President Emerita of Goddard College, and she is director and professor of Integrated Studies at California State University in Monterey Bay. She works as a dramaturge, actor, keynoter, and literary critic, performing internationally as a senior Fulbright lecturer and U.S. State Department speaker/consultant. Her book *Emily Dickinson: When a Writer Is a Daughter* (Indiana, 1983) was named Choice Outstanding Academic Book of the Year.

Steven Paschall holds a bachelor's degree in English Literature and Writing from the University of Colorado in Denver. He teaches American literature and the English language at Lycée St. Sigisbert in Nancy, France, where is also doing graduate studies at l'Université de Lorraine. In addition to writing, he is a musician and photographer. His first poetry collection *Polaroids* was selected for the Patricia Bibby Award and published in 2009 by Tebot Bach.

Susanna Rich has been an Emmy Award nominee and a Fulbright Fellow in Creative Writing. She is author of two Finishing Line Press chapbooks: *Television Daddy* (2008) and *The Drive Home* (2009). She founded Wild Nights Productions, through which she tours audience-interactive, poetry experiences including *ashes, ashes: A Poet Responds to the Holocaust*; *Television Daddy*; *The Drive Home*; and *A Wild Night with Emily Dickinson*. She is a professor of English at Kean University and was awarded the Presidential Excellence Award for Distinguished Teaching. (www.susannarich.com)

Liz Robbins's *Play Button* won the 2010 Cider Press Review Book Award, judged by Patricia Smith. Her poems are forthcoming in *Cimarron Review*, *The Journal*, and *New York Quarterly*. She is an assistant professor of creative writing at Flagler College in St. Augustine, Florida.

Aubrey Ryan's work has appeared recently or will soon in *Best New Poets 2011, Quarterly West, Booth, Squat Birth Journal,* and *Cellpoems.* She lives in Iowa with her husband and their son, who she calls "the best muse of all."

Jo Anne Valentine Simson, an erstwhile anatomist, has published poetry and short stories using the name V. Pascoe (Valentine Pascoe, a combination of her maiden name and that of her mother), mostly in local publications, although one of her stories was published in *Kansas Quarterly* and a few poems have been published in the journal *Perspectives in Biology and Medicine.*

Molly Spencer is a poet, an avid reader of poetry and almost anything else, and a mother of three. Her work has appeared in *Literary Mama, Linebreak, CALYX,* and elsewhere. A native Michigander and temporary Minnesotan, she now lives in the San Francisco Bay Area with her husband and their children. She blogs about poetry and the writing life at http://mollyspencer.wordpress.com/.

Jeneva Stone's poems and nonfiction have appeared in the *Beloit Poetry Journal, Colorado Review, The Collagist, RHINO,* and many others. She is the recipient of 2012 fellowships from the MacDowell and Millay Colonies for her memoir about a disabled son's undiagnosed illness. She most hopes, though, that you will respect her in the morning.

Judith Terzi's poetry has received nominations for Best of the Net and Web as well as recognition and awards from various journals and presses. Recent work is forthcoming in *BorderSenses, CHEST Journal, FutureCycle* ("American Society: What Poets See"), *Jewish Women's Literary Annual, Poemeleon,* and elsewhere. For many years a high school French teacher, she also taught English at California State University, Los Angeles, and in Algiers, Algeria. Her book *Sharing Tabouli* was published by Finishing Line Press in 2011.

Gail Thomas has published two books, *No Simple Wilderness: An Elegy for Swift River Valley* (Haley's, 2000) and *Finding the Bear* (Perugia Press, 1997). Her poems have appeared in many journals including the *Beloit Poetry Journal, Calyx, Hanging Loose, The North American Review, The Chiron Review,* and *Cider Press Review.* She has been awarded residencies at the MacDowell Colony and the Ucross Foundation, and individual poems from her newest manuscript have won the Pat Schneider Prize and the James Hearst Prize.

Kim Triedman's first poetry collection, *bathe in it or sleep*, won the 2008 Main Street Rag Chapbook Competition; in the past few years she's won or been shortlisted in over ten additional poetry and fiction competitions. She is also the developer and editor of *Poets for Haiti: An Anthology of Art* (Yileen Press, 2010). She is a graduate of Brown University and is currently the managing editor of *Ibbetson Street Review*.

Bruce Willard's poems have appeared in *Connotation Press: An Online Artifact*, *Harvard Review*, *Mead Magazine*, *Salamander*, *5 AM*, and other publications. His first collection of poems, *Holding Ground*, is due out from Four Way Books in Spring 2013. He is a graduate of Middlebury College and of Bennington College's M.F.A. program. He works in the clothing business and lives with his family in California and Maine.

P. Ivan Young is the author of *A Shape in the Waves* (Stepping Stones Press, 2009) and a recipient of a 2011 Individual Artist Award from the Maryland State Arts Council. His most recent publications are in the anthology *Challenges for the Delusional* as well as in *Zone 3*, *The Summerset Review*, *Crab Orchard Review*, and *Barnwood*. He teaches at Salisbury University in Maryland, where he lives with his wife and two children.

Editors

Marie Gauthier is Director of Sales & Marketing of Tupelo Press and the author of a chapbook, *Hunger All Inside* (Finishing Line Press, 2009). Recent poems can be read or are forthcoming in *The Common*, *Cave Wall*, *Salamander*, and *Poetry Northwest*. She won a 2008 Dorothy Sargent Rosenberg Poetry Prize in addition to Honorable Mention for that prize in 2010. She co-curates the Collected Poets Series in Shelburne Falls, Massachusetts.

Jeffrey Levine is the author of two books: *Rumor of Cortez*, nominated for a 2006 Los Angeles Times Literary Award in Poetry, and *Mortal, Everlasting*, which won the 2002 Transcontinental Poetry Prize. A graduate of the Warren Wilson M.F.A. Program for Writers, he is founder, Editor-in-Chief, and Publisher of Tupelo Press.

Acknowledgments

Two of the poems in this collection were previously published
and they are used by permission:

"New" by Amy MacLennan is from *Weathering*,
published by Utter Chaos Press;
copyright 2012 Amy MacLennan.

"Drought" by Kim Triedman is from *bathe in it or sleep*,
published by Main Street Rag;
copyright 2008 Kim Triedman.

Other Books from Tupelo Press

See our complete backlist at
www.tupelopress.org

CPSIA information can be obtained at www.ICGtesting.com
Printed in the USA
BVOW02s0534100216

435652BV00008B/228/P